She Wrote Her Own Eulogy
Shirley May

She Wrote Her Own Eulogy
Shirley May

ISBN 978-1-9031106-3-8

First published by Wrecking Ball Press 2018.

Design by humandesign.co.uk

Supported using public funding by
ARTS COUNCIL ENGLAND
LOTTERY FUNDED

Dedicated to

Edith Elizabeth Phillips Clarke
and Kingbell Benjamin Phillips

I would like to dedicate this book to my parents who came to the UK in the '50s; to my husband of 32 years, Winston; to my children, Alexander and Nicole May who kept on saying, 'Please, just press send'; and to my siblings who always support my work, Shako Diesa and my grandchildren, and a special thank you to my big sister, Marcia (Phillips Clarke) Bryan who never misses an event if she can help it. I do thank God that I come from a sizeable Caribbean family network—you are the best!

Thanks to the rest of my family and friends who have supported events and poetry readings over many years. It's here!

I would like to thank Peter Kalu and *Cultureword*, who helped edit some of the poems, alongside Desiree Reynolds and Tolu Agbelusi. All of your points were valid, and you have helped with my process even if I did not always agree with you.

A massive thanks goes to Reece Williams and Isaiah Hull who laid the book out on my living room floor and said, 'You got something'; and to Dionne Marland, who took my scraps and my old notebooks, and tried to decipher my handwriting—well done.

I want to thank Sue Roberts for her massive encouragement after she read the manuscript. Thank you to Louise Wallwein MBE, Sonia Hughes, Sharon Raymond, Sidnie Pantry, Chris Nelson, Ali Gadema, and Segun Lee French for always being my poetry family.

A special thanks to *Speakeasy* people, and *Young Identity* and *Inna Voice* poetry collectives, all of whom I have helped to manage.

Thanks, also, to Shane Rhodes and the team at Wrecking Ball Press.

And - finally - my besties, Flo Wilson, Ian Bobb, Christine Perry and Mira Williams, and the late Dikè Omeje, R.I.P.: my friends from forever. They said they loved my work, my voice, my poetry, and me, whatever the condition I come in: *"you could read the telephone directory and we would love it."* I will forever be grateful because of your encouragement.

FOREWORD

'Mi mother always used to seh...' Shirley May has often started a sentence so, over the years that I have known her. The sentence usually ends, as many a Caribbean mother's sayings would end in a poetic yet elusive riddle, one which leaves you scratching your head but nevertheless repeating. In your twenties you begin to unravel and translate the saying. But it's not until your middle years that you truly recognise the lived wisdom in the words passed down.

Maybe this is why it's taken Shirley May so blasted long to write this damn book! Perhaps she had to wait for the wisdom to accrue to be certain enough of her mother's words to commit them to print. In any case, it's been a long time in the belly. Long overdue, certainly; but finally, and happily, it's here.

And, so, hungry, I open the book. It begins with the heartache and dreaming of those first-generation migrants in *Tunbridge Wells*. I have heard my family's versions of these stories—most Caribbean migrants have similar tales to tell. But it's not just a reminiscence. *Not All Of Us Came On The Windrush* draws a gasp: it's a meditation, a sadness, and a miniature revelation of how life can be. A revelation which, as I said, can only be truly grasped as life moves on.

For years, Shirley has told me snippets of stories from 285 Moss Lane East, the house she grew up in, a way-station for new-comers from the Caribbean. The drinking den in the basement; West Indian men and British women mingling for the first time; Big Shirley, who in my memory was called Man Shirley. I never grew up in a house like that - I was brought up in suburbia - but it reminded me of the Henrys, or my Uncle Cecil's pig foot in the pot, coloured shot glasses, Saturday dominos shindig. Here, it comes to light with all the tangled innards of the thing, especially in *Mother B's Establishment* and *Big Shirley* - Red Trunk. The light and the shade; the one can only exist with the other.

As well as painting scenes and telling stories, Shirley draws close and creates intimate portraits of people living with ambivalence and torture, both equally detrimental to a soul, in *Complicit, Delilah's House Monton Street*, and *The Man Who Had No Sentences Left In Him*, and I'm set to wondering how the casual brutality of being out of place can utterly dismantle a person.

All this I'm glad for, though. I remember when I first met Shirley May, before I'd even thought of putting pen to paper. She was performing poetry at my son's school at a launch for a family writing project. I don't remember what she said, but I remember her. Commanding and mellifluous. Long curly hair, a seductive performer; I had a slight trepidation when she asked me to write this. What if her poems had been nothing more than simple lullabies which sounded delightful when spoken aloud, but offered nothing more than twee rhymes when written down? Oh, me of little faith.

One of the things I really love about Shirley, though, is her Christianity. I admire what I perceive to be her struggle with it, her boiling questioning of it and then her calm reliance upon it. She seems to be always in pursuit of faith, in the true sense of practising it. This collection is laced with Bible references, but her battles are also on show in *Close To The Pit*. Despite my admiration, I'm remained an Atheist, and in *Gather Unto Me I Say* she shows me how and why me must still be friends.

In any case, there's a lot of sex in these poems. Good sex and bad sex, rape definitely, child abuse probably. But luscious moments, too, which for me evokes Janie sitting under the pear tree watching the bees in Zora Neale Hurtson's. And, Lord knows, Shirley May is a sensuous woman—read *Silvered Moon Man*. Or maybe I should say, Shirley's mother was a sensuous woman, for that man was released in some way from her mother's journal.

I never met Shirley's Mum, but I went to her funeral. I missed the service - probably on purpose - and went straight to the cemetery. My memory is of Shirley at the head of her mother's grave, leading the singing as though she were the eldest. My mother was still alive at that point, so I didn't yet know how you could listen to earth falling onto your Mum's coffin and be not crying but singing.

Shirley is a lot more practised at funerals than I am. She goes to so many because she has gathered so many people to her. People who are not casual acquaintances, but people she knows the hearts of, people with whom she has stood alongside, with whom she has drunk, danced, laughed, prayed; and, with her artist's heart, observed.

With all that dancing and dying, but most of all living, she has let the time pass when she should have been writing. Although, of course, she has always been writing, whilst visiting the sick, nurturing burgeoning talent and young souls, persuading the temporarily hopeless that life is worth living, holding down jobs, battling for funding, running workshops, throwing parties, and feeding her family and friends and all who pass by her door. I used to say that her and Winston's home was like the Cosby house. Unfortunately, that's no longer a good thing. But it was.

Shirley May has been writing all along, not with a pen but with a mind that's been sifting, shaking out the gaudy lumps, picking out the tight knots. For all my consternation I think that the passing of time was necessary. Alongside deeper understanding, we have become less afraid of the truth, less fearful of others' censure. Less afraid of our own rage. There are a number of poems in this collection which sing out against injustice: White against Black, rich against poor, men against women, women against women. They are big targets which can become trite if not examined closely, if the hurts are generalised and the ambiguity of an individual's actions are not explored. With the perspective of time, Shirley May has studied the minutiae and can write with all of the rage and clarity that she can muster.

This is Shirley May's gift.

I am writing this on the day of Aretha Franklin's death and after just taking leave of my father, who by his own admission is going 'tatty in the head'. He has Alzheimer's. These two things are reminders for me that as we lose our Queens and our direct-from-the-soil memories of the Caribbean, we must laud the royalty amongst us and hold on tight to our collective memories.

Thanks, Shirl.

Sonia Hughes, Artist.

Sometimes the most complicated lives need to be explained in the simplest of ways. I always aim for high ground, taking no captives.

My cousin, Judith Clarke, said, 'Bitterness changes your countenance, so laugh and smile all day—you will remain beautiful.'

Shirley May

CONTENTS

SHE MADE ME LOVE JAMAICA

SHE WROTE HER OWN EULOGY

MY GRANDMOTHER'S STORY

TUNBRIDGE WELLS

NOT ALL OF US CAME ON THE WINDRUSH

My mother once told me that, in her old age,
she travelled to England first class. Ate at the captain's table
and danced with Sidney Poitier on a ship called the Queen Mary.

She said thus, dreaming was not just the pursuit of the young.
I want to remind you, value your time.
It runs away with your life.

THE WILSONS

It's funny how life can shift so quickly.
When you look after other people's children
and lose sight of your own, it nuh easy,
this place sees only my skin, back home it was not the case.
Well, not in the countryside,
where the life of the sugarcane is what most men knew.
And the homestead is what a girl is taught at birth.
She, like her mother, had been once accepting of this
state; she said even a country girl dreams of escaping the
mundane.

Sister and Honey they called me, it not my name, I own both
like they were my birth names. I wear them on different days.
Sister at home, where the work is hard for the sixth child, in the
middle of twelve.
Honey is my Sunday name, it's what my grandmother Rosina
called me,
she made me special, she taught me to love myself,
like she was taught by my mother.

I don't know how I ended up in England; it was not my intention.
It's funny how life can shift so quickly.
Mr & Mrs Wilson, whose children Polly and Douglas
are my wards, said they had been assigned to England.
Did I want to come, as they knew New York was the reason I took
the job.
I said, no, I'll go home, I had a good life there,
only ended up in Tunbridge Wells because Polly and Douglas
wouldn't stop crying.
It's funny how life can shift so quickly.

I was only in America eight weeks.
By then I knew I was pregnant again, so I came to England.
Do you nuh mi mind, Polly and Douglas two more years?
Fe mi children placed in the care of the state,
who did not know how to care dem.

MOSS SIDE

MOTHER B'S ESTABLISHMENT

285 Moss Lane East.
You could feel home.
It was the aroma of good vibes
and patois laced tongues.

Mother B's establishment
where Harry Belafonte's "Oh, island in the sun"
was on repeat, you couldn't help
but love her cornmeal porridge,
2-hour dumplings, stew peas and rice,
salt pork on your lips. Irish Moss
and Guinness punch that came with a warning,
helped a brother kiss right.

She rented rooms for the night,
would descend into the cellar
turn on the red light, set up the bar.
Her house was the spot
after the Reno was shut.

People would come from far and wide to sway
to the rhythms of the night; Persian di music man
played John Holt, 'Cupid draw back your bow,
you know love will find a way.'

White women with red lips
auburn, brunette and golden came
with powdered faces, like locusts
on new crops, she said; devouring men
from holy places like St Ann, St Elizabeth

And Mama's St Catherine.

They came to school these men
in the ways of the slender-hipped woman
with small breasts and exotic northern tongues
helping them to forget
the wives and children they left behind
waiting for them to return.

Shaking her head slowly,
she would descend into the cellar
turn on the red light, set up the bar.
Her house was the spot
after the Reno was shut.

People would come from far and wide to sway
to the rhythms of the night; Persian di music man
played Jimmy Cliff, "Many rivers to cross."

She whispered her memory in my ear.

BIG SHIRLEY - RED TRUNK

I
I am trying to decide what I should keep.
I come across photographs she took when coming to England,
the papers with his name change from Maurice to Maureen
though we called her Big Shirley. There was everything
in that red trunk at the bottom of her bed.
It was a tumble of yesterday's promises,
tomorrows never come.

II
It was six flights up into her room.
By the time I turned the door handle
I was panting.
She kept a trunk just at the bottom
of her bed. Not one of those silver coloured ones
with the bronze bolted ends
that everybody coming from the island
seemed to have for their return.
Hers was bright red melamine. It had a strange
textured feel, not smooth, a bit like her,
so many things packed tightly.

I don't know why there was a pressure cooker
in there but I knew she was under the kind of pressure
you could never conceive.
As him-she, I heard people say, then laugh and turn away.
In that trunk were razors to take the stubble from her chin,
shave the hair between her cleavage.
There was a flower bed spread of candlewick pink,
ten marinas and five boxers bought for grandpa
and now faded with age.

The doctor declared her identity "hermaphrodite"
delivered the news of her cancer to me carelessly
as if she meant nothing to no one. I don't know when she
packed
the trunk, but she never made it back home.

LIFE IS VAST

So he sleeps blind, then he is boxed,
remembering no man knows the truth,
only his own reality.
The day comes, the day goes
it is unholy where the mind doth wonder.
No small moment is that small,
for once we think, it is vast,
sometimes it can seem unfathomable.

THE MAN WHO HAD NO
SENTENCES LEFT IN HIM

This man—stopping father from beating me once; I loved him
until his final breath.

The story goes,
that a woman destroyed him.
By the time I knew him
he had no sentences left in him.

I was only five when he came.
My eyes were full of his size,
the dirt and decay that fused to him.
The smell of him made me gasp.

Water, my mother softly called.
She said, "Put your feet in here,
soak and wash them.
Let your feet once again feel, free."

His eyes filled with tears at the pain
and the kindness he found there.
As Mother B bent down to wash his feet,
she peeled away at his socks and
his flesh mingled there, his blood shed.

I saw the anger rise within her.
"Why?" The question came, who had caused
this decay and pain, to so tall and handsome
a black man, on God's good day.

Memory lingers on a friend.
The man who had no sentences left in him.
His silence was his own,
no one could reach to the pain concealed there.
Mama said, some questions had no answers,
some things needed to be left alone.

As a child I loved him,
as a teenager I wanted to bring him back
to those who cared.
Had I known his time was short
I would have tried harder.

He never revealed who caused his hurt.
At his funeral, I imagine I heard
the soil that fell, sing his song.

COMPLICIT

His mother dressed me.
Bought me for him.
The cake, rich.
The ceremony long.
I too will try to please.
Too afraid of change,
now I have a daughter for sale.

DELILAH'S HOUSE MONTON STREET

The Queen's Mother taught her daughter to dance that she might
behead a man
All things can be taught in one season.

Bang, bang, bang.
Just let me bend you this way then that!
It's March and we can do this till December.
Bang, bang, bang bang
And yes I am bent double, there is no tenderness.
No words sweet, just sweating and grunting and gritting of teeth.
This new position makes my leg go dead and my mind numb.
It's January and the twins are about to be born.

Bang bang, bang,
the nurse calls for forceps.
And yes my legs are up in the air again;
there is no tenderness, no words sweet,
just sweating and gritting and more grunting.
And my back hurts and
it's spring and this work is too hard,
my mother said it's honest work,
my spirit does not believe her.

It's March again,
Bang, bang, bang,
the twins were made by sex; I will not love them less—
they grew in me. They are mine and I theirs
and that is how it should be,
that's what my mother said
whilst taking the money from my last trick.

My Yugoslavian mother gave me the key to the brothel and told me
it was my turn, to turn the key in the lock,
for there be many a tricks, in her game.

And she had taught me them all,
and yes it was March again and the twins are now four,
and I have not named them yet.
They were made from sex.
I was hoping their father, Mr. X, might come back,
and together we would name them but still we wait.

Bang, bang, bang.

ROMPFRORD X EMPLOYEE

Rompfrord employee
work colleague
yellow man
dutty man
want to turn you out
when you just a grow.
When womanhood is ripening
yet nobody say nothing
but everybody know.

He love ya when see you a blossom,
him sai your titty them a grow like bud,
he sai soon you can take man,
hee hee hee hee hee hee.

Spring's new sapling him want to fel.
He will tell ya sa he will cook you a little food
rice and peas, with freshly grated coconut,
one small clove garlic, mashed to nothing.
Two sweet peppers chopped fine and small.

Fe help colour de water, red.
A pinch of black pepper fe add fire,
Bring it to the boil, like him going bring you to the boil
him say, then simmer until it dry out,
hee hee hee hee hee hee.

Chopper in hand him slice deep into the flesh of spring bird.
Sai he don't want no boiler chicken.
It's too old and fowl,

and can't lay egg anymore,
it smell might be sweet but its meat is tough.
Him a look for an easy laying bird.
One easy to chop and roast.

So him prepare the new harvest wid sweet things
like coconut drops, paradise plums, mint balls and de sweetest festival
and let mi not fe get de Silver sixpence.
While adjusting himself in de crouches
he looking at you while you a try fe look away,
him call you to come to him kitchen
placing his warm yet damp hands
over yours, pressing down on top,
he cuts deep into the flesh.
Skin, bone and blood, shatter under that pressure.
His thoughts now audible, mi can show
any man how; to quarter this yah chicken.
Hee hee hee.

JUDGE NOT LEST YE BE JUDGED

My mother taught me to love my friends and neighbours.
Even if their life style was not one of de *cloth*,
she hoped her children would pursue righteousness,
even though there were occasions when she was not practising,
she said, mothers always wanted something different for their
children.

I WAS MADE FROM LOVE AND
MY MOTHER'S TEARS

Dedicated to Doreen Patrick.

On the night I was conceived
bodies crashed against each other,
they were like fire and lava in their shuddering climax—
I was made Jamaican in that moment.
Born in the belly of rainy season, April.
I am just a Black woman here
and an English woman there.

In the nine months she carried me
I listened to the sounds of 1962
hearing her voice and that of my father
learning, her language, her laughter.
I ate sweet potato and stew peas and rice,
drank carrot juice and ginger tea,
I knew when she ate "hell a bottom hell a top
and hallelujah in de middle" pudding.
It was always followed by a heavenly sigh
like it made her forget her mother was dying
and I was about to be born.

I could hear my sister Doreen, she was three
I knew her voice too. Not much to do for nine months
but listen. She sang songs with Mr Brown,
songs like *Row The Boat Gently Down The Stream,*
Big Girls Don't Cry
and *You Don't Know Me.*

She whispered to my mother's belly,
she was Jamaican too. It was in her nuances,
it was the fire in her spirit, the loudness of her scream.
I heard her tantrums,
they were glorious.
Teaching me the way even before I had my own
and I knew I loved her.

I heard her tell Mummy she could not wait
for me any longer, that she was to hurry up.
Fifty years later,
she helps me ease the loss of
you who made me Jamaican in your forties.

NEXT

She held me gripped between her legs, I leaned
into the familiar smell of freshly chopped

thyme, curry and seasoning and raw meat
still lingering on her clothes and hands.

Mama's wash belly[1] was first, the youngest
and luckiest of five girls. She turned my head

as though it was a mechanism separate
from my neck and shoulders. I jerk back

she manoeuvres me in her vice like grip
between her large thighs and began to part my hair.

I hummed familiar tunes, echoes between each ouch
and why are you pulling so hard?

Her reply incoherent, laced with rasss
and another *Jesus is my saviour*, as she combed

through knots and then brushed I often wondered
why she did not brush then comb

(my own daughter asked me that question).
Turn to me, she said. The best position to be in

closest to her smell. You could cradle
your head in her lap, tended with love and hate

both at the same time. She called out
to the second to last child for the white ribbon

two huge bows either side of my head
She shouted, *Finished. Next.*

[1] *wash belly: a mother's last child*

SHE TOLD HER DAUGHTERS STORIES ABOUT MEN AND WOMEN

DI ROAD THAT LEADS TO A BAD MAN'S BED

My mother use to say he dat keepeth him mouth, keepeth him life!
There is a time and a place fi all things.
Give me di bwoy till him 45 and we might see a grown up at 70.
You never too old fi learn di path to righteous living!
Narrow is the way to life eternal and broad is di road that lead to
di badman's bed.

SILVERED MOON MAN

Mummy said moon-water
was for lovers, that reflected you
as were the lights that spit shine
in the sky on July in Jamaica.
It was not for little girls, she said.

Not even big women knew how to handle themselves
when the moon shone full, danger lingered
and other things stained the air
like a natural misty malevolent musk.
She said she would bequeath me her journal,

her roadmap on how to move in the forest,
where darkened things hid in places
the night's light did not penetrate
to share itself on pathways of skin and sinew.
She said that sometimes truth was on the lips of lovers.

At these times, men's fingers stumbled in caverns
where the moon cast silver imprints on dampened bodies
and the grass stained your buttocks and elbows in
valley places and soft areas where bodies collided
and made new generations. My mum spoke

of peninsula trembled earthquakes shaking
water, blood and strong men beholding replicas
of themselves being born.
There would be a time when I would know
the world of secrets within its pages.

She said holdfast, for she had bequeathed me
her journal that remembered
July in Jamaica, moon-water
and love making.

ALL THE SUNFLOWERS HAVE GONE

Blazing with emotion that left you depleted.
Signs of a hard life engraved
in every line of your face.
Convulsing, swaying, sweating as you dance
him out of your soul
only to wake and find you are mourning.

The one who painted Van Gogh sunflowers in your life
but stole all your sunshine.

It takes a long time for nothing to be left.
Now nothing remains except for the kids,
they change hands every weekend.

HIS AFRO LOCKS GLISTEN

I sit here longing.

You hold court,
the most noble
subjects laid waste in the dirt.
Discarded play things.

Pretended you were never beautiful
yet, walking past mirrors,
you strike a pose.

End of sentence, you lick
the corners of your mouth.
Your tongue wilts pink,
co-conspirator,
a cavern of testimony and slander.

You remain always aloof.

Moon on open waters,
deep
black
pools,
you sunder your willing victims.
Afro locks glisten
on pale opaque skin.
You swear she is your queen,
your new mooring.

THEN SHE WAS

Draped in leaves of green, the Lady of the Garland.
Gossamer reflecting the sun,
it shone on her like a hundred thousand lights of love.
She's descending, swaying,
each step in time to the rhythms of lights.
They cling to her,
life fading only with the rings that now encircled her eyes.
Longing for release she sailed
onto a new plain where becoming knows her name.
She grows with the knowledge of the first temptation,
the task was hers,
as the liquid of her lust drips from the corners of her mouth;
the knowledge did not free her,
though scales fell from her eyes.

Now she knows the pain of loving, it sweats her body.
It's on her face, glistening,
as she wails in birth.
Only a faded memory of Eden remains.
She emanates with new knowing,
her mind filling instantly.
He harkens unto her,
smelling the change even before he partakes of the same.
He cries out her name,

Eve! Woman! Bone of my bone, flesh of my flesh. I will descend,
for the smell of your fruit
holds me,
like the jester I dance at your table,

she says you are most welcome.

Then their eyes were opened and they knew they were naked
so they hid from God.
And some of us are still hiding!

The tree of knowledge of good and evil.[2]

[2] *Genesis 2:9*

WHEN YOU'RE UNABLE TO SLEEP

For Graham Phillips Clarke (AKA Papa G) and Davina Webb

Part One

Schooling in his eyes was the metamorphosis
they hoped to achieve.
Only he was not receptive to the rhythms of their voice,
so he grew in rebellion and learned to rebel.
To seek a new intelligence from someone,
from elsewhere,
from the men of his clan,
from the women who bore him.
He would not propagate their lies
nor allow flowers to bloom in infertile soil.

Part Two

Schooling in her eyes was the metamorphosis
they hoped to achieve.
Only she was not receptive to the rhythms of their voice,
so she grew in rebellion and learned to rebel.
To seek a new intelligence from someone,
from elsewhere,
from the men of her clan,
from the women who bore her.
She would not propagate their lies
nor allow flowers to bloom in infertile soil,
For the soul of a woman in a not for sale.

VIXEN SAID MI AUNTY

She's a sister but a traitor to the cause, or is she?
With legs up to her larynx,
bust size equaling twin peaks.
She flutters her eyelashes and smiles
when she thinks they're looking,
pretends to feel a little unsure, insecure
but you and I know her.
We have heard her sisterly rap and she is on the hunt now,
a man she will trap.
Just like the black widow.
She tempts her victims
with a promise of loving sweetness
that knows no end.
She invites you to enter her sticky web.
Eats meat at her leisure until only the waste remains.
Then she moves on to the next meal
feasting on those in her path
who don't want to see the games she plays.
She is a vixen, that won't be tamed.

RAIN FALL

She was yours to overwhelm,
you were even more afraid than her.
When your essence connected
you ran for cover,
hid all emotion from your eyes.
Found drink your friend,
loveless love your lover.
You, the victim in your own demise,
full on in to destruction, your isolation,
so you hunger for the truth
that you long gave up.
That thing
"El Elyon"[3]
you could not sense her touch,
the brush of her leg against you,
only the roughness of the cloth
that you used to shield yourself.
Could not find tenderness in her,
always
looking for dishonesty
in whomever draws close
even in
"The Most High".
Measuring her
from your own pandemonium,
never looking for that which overwhelms you,
you sought your executioner,
your incarceration was your own making.
You now wonder from place to place
fatal attractions in smoky places

to help in your deconstruction.
Love came from unexpected places,
you kept it at arms' length
just in case it consumes you,
not the easy love that rolls
off the lips of just-met acquaintances.
But the love that drives the air from your lungs
at first seeing,
the love that comes from pure wanting
the love that turns into familiar
places and contours.
The love comes from
"El Elyon".
There were no pistols drawn at day break
from an offended lover,
just you in the race.
You and
"The Most High".

---

[3] *'El Elyon' is a Hebrew epithet given to God meaning 'The Most High'.*

I HAVE A NEW HYMN THAT I SING

Olive Marland: A sister with her own kind of wisdom.

I want to smile daily, taking no hostages.
I seek no revenge,
I will navigate my problems when I encounter them.
Looking for Utopia is a good thing.

ARE WE STILL BETRAYED?

Friendship, so I thought.
She was rich molasses—
Blood blue, royal.
My hope is to be replaced by you.
For you are the future and I the past.
Did I ever show envy of your status?
Did I lust for your youth?
Or did I encourage you?
So why do I still cry?
Why do I still cry?

Greed, jealousy, they are no longer for me.
Have as much as you want,
have as much as you need.
But heed my warning,
you will still feel incomplete.

Rich molasses, blood blue.
I hope more for you.
So why do I still cry?
Why do I still cry?

Wise was the woman who told me this.
She said,
"Evolve and be what we could not be,
aim for higher ground,
look for no victims,
take no captives.
For you are the future,
I am the past

and you are holding the key to everything
that we could not be.
Let there be no more tears".

WHO SAID BLOOD WAS THICK

Who said blood was thick
with remembering,
and water
the substance of nothing?

Yet on bended knee,
did change water into the choicest of wines.
Leaving you in no doubt.

When the hand of the divine give
quarter. Then why not your bone,
your flesh, are we not blood?

Yet you turn with disdain from those
whose lineage and DNA you share,
losing so much from our many facets.

How grand and lonely is the place on the mountains?
Where the altitude is thin, leaving men sick,
confused, in their loftiness.

Can you turn money into blood?
Or erase the memory of sarcophagus ships,
let's give thanks for those who survived for us.

My granny left me a warning; *wear your freedom*
like good Sunday clothes and leave the field ones
for the remaining weak days.

Water and wine can drown you,
while blood holds the essence of your spirit and life.
And family be the crown you own.
Remember to guard it and treat it like a precious thing.

Let not your beginning also be your journey's end.
For it's on the turning,
that the most important can be lost
to stubbornness you're bearing.
Once those who loved you are gone,
your words of rejection cannot be undone,
it's like liquorice on your tongue.
Just a lucid memory of how it used to be.
How it once tasted.

THE PRICE IS ETERNAL

For Alexander May.

There is only amen and amen,
the race is short; the eternal is infinite.
And there are no time lords.

Just time and the spirit of angels,
who are often the women, the men we know.
So pursue your dream and live your life
with your purpose in mind.

BIO-DEGRADABLE MAN

Bio - de grade a bull man.
Dirt ingrained in skin and clothes
the knots of your dreads tell
their own incorporate story.
You walk. The Magnificent Mile,
of North Michigan Avenue.
Dwarfed by skylines
in Downtown Chicago,
where the Sears Tower doesn't see
there will be no shearing,
of those locks today.
No corporate welcome team.
For the reflection of this man, my brother, my father, my son.
Bio - de grade a bull man.
Ingenious are the Cardboard shoes
you wear and the madness that is home.
Momma did not remember
your name at your birth,
nor your father's name after the first night.
Begging change in the city of the president
whilst street corner living, you roam
clawed toed. Navigating, these Cityscapes,
knowing there's no breakfast at Tiffany's
for the stinking, not even a back door.
Chicago, whose blood diamonds are you draped in?
Bio - de grade a bull man.
The Invisible existence you move in
we try not to see,
your hollowed out eyes, and thinning jaw line
absolve me of this responsibility.

I've come to shop,
arid eyes in my staring,
you remind me of the hungry in India and Africa.
Bio - de grade a bull man.
In downtown, we hide our eyes from the evidence
and see no sign; hear not the sound, of your song,
blank vacancy. Careless. We care less, desolate is the truth,
this world is not third
nor second
but first.
To the men on every corner of this city, Chicago,
heat and hate flourish, there's no fields of poppies,
nor remembrance.
Just the missing
Bio - de grade a bull man.
Degrading an able man.

THE BOY HAD DREAMS

For Victor Daniels

The boy had dreams of orange suns
and darker days.
He laughs at the light that's in your eyes
as sure as death he knows it will fade away,
in the morning of the midnight dreams
at the dawning of another workday.

His laughter is like a whip on the back,
he knows they hold the handle,
and you hold the blade, if drawn, your blood,
will fall like a crimson rain.

Mama said you cannot sit around
hoping for revolution, or you will be like
a memory that fades,
crushed under foot like the autumn leaves,
discarded by the season change,
so her advice to all,
was seize your tomorrows
in the dawning of every new day.

DONE HERE

She taught them that they hold life in water jars,
to dream big not small,
to be the master of your own
four walls. To leave an imprint
for those to come, that they too,
would be rewarded by their own hands.

THE SCARRED MAN

In remembrance of Ben, my dad.

You noticed them right away.
The scars that are not new,
markings on my Father's face.
I thought you Jamaican,
a long lost Africa,
what is your lost heritage my B?
Glass sandpaper is my tongue
stuck to the roof of my mouth.
You want to question,
you want answers,
but this is your father and you born, sixth child.
Conceived in the sexual revolution.

Yet your tongue is held back,
like a child in the 1800s,
speak when you're spoken to.
Put on the 6 o'clock news.
His authority is a switch that spoke to the wind
and crackle, cutting the air before reaching skin.
Also a belt hanging on ugly nail
on the wall with a cross beside it,
his mark of 10.
His authority is never questioned
we comply like robots
trained in a discipline that is Jamaican.

A BLOODY STREAM ON
A DIRT ROAD INTO TOWN

He walked weightlessly
peacocking, in tar stained khaki.
Laughing loudly, dancing backwards
and forwards, excited, joyous,
she walked with him from her village.

It was hot. Like when the waxy oil
of yourself sits on your skin,
because the heat of this land
is high in God's creation.
She didn't mind him sing to her.
Didn't care that her dampness was visible.

That pleasure too, she was full to the top with it,
it was in her laughter, as she planned her future with his brother.
He pushed her off the open road
into the gulley below, just outside
of town. Unafraid, he t'rew her down.

He smelt of brimstone and bitumen
from the road he just laid. He had hummed
and sung "my baby just cares for me"
as they laughed together moments before.
But now, snorting, squealing and swearing,
he eradicating her purity.

Shovelling the seed of his first child
into her, it oozes down her legs
as she tried to stand, wondering how
she would tell his brother.

Salted tears and a yellow purple blueness
stain her cheekbones, her new white dress,
like her, ripped, bent double, blistered
lips cracked open and sour as her screams scraped
the air and no one heard. His wickedness witnessed by only
John Crow perched
in tree, waiting to eat dead meat. And that song,
he kept singing that song "my baby just cares for me".

A bloody stream, ran down her legs.
Warm at first, then cold. The bitumen
that lingered on him, now on her
burned into her nostrils
with the memory of an open road.

In the aftermath, there was stillness.
For half a century, Nana pretended to forget.
Walking down the road, one day she jerked,
held her nose, her breath,
as though she was being poisoned. "I hate that smell."
"What smell?" I asked as she held me. I held her back.

Could sense her spirit howling
like a she wolf's warning. Body shaking,
at 70, Nana told me her story
her memories, a lamentation, a spectre.
We walked the rest of the journey in silence
smelling the newly asphalted road to her home.

SHE MADE ME LOVE JAMAICA

DREAMING OF JAMAICA

For Enid and Eric Phillips: the passing of time has no signature.

I just want to walk on a beach,
think only about the cacophony of sea meeting shore.
The sunset orange to midnight,
the freedom to love and it not be misinterpreted as weakness,
to throw away the shoes of constraint and to sit awhile.

MISS IMMIGRATION

A fi we, dis place, I feel it
like I feel a body pressed
up against me, reassuring me
that only death will separate us now.
Your sunshine kisses more than my skin,
feeds me, you burn deep, singeing
me to the Jamaican earth.

"What is your purpose on this
occasion on my island,
who have yuh cum fe see?"

"Visit wid mi people, relax a while,
you know, ordinary."

I smile. She does not return
my efforts to make light conversation.

Mama used to say
bad manners reflected upon her,
so be well-mannered and civil,
it could earn you a paradise plum
or a mint ball
and not a beating.

Only if Mama was truly upset,
did Jamaican swearwords
came out of she mout—
yet she never quite abandoned her stateliness—
even then.

No eye to eye contact
from Miss Immigration, wid she badmind self.
No acknowledgement
dat dis ya sista had returned,
nothing but another question
"What's in de bag?"
"Nothing but mi clothes.
Everything in my heart, though."

Still I hear my Mama's voice
in my head.
"Harsh words stir up strife
while soft words turn away wrath.
He that keepeth his mouth, keepeth his life."

I reeled off the list of bad word
that had briefly invaded my mind—
They all ended in clart,
but I made no utterance.
Without warning, Miss Immigration
threw me a curve ball—wide like de ocean
we did just cross
she smiled!
"Enjoy your stay in Jamaica
and spend spend spend... and spend!"

I'm glad I'm here.
You see, I know some of your angles look
a little tired in places
and you coulda smartened up
because you knew I was coming
but, I don't mind—
Mama taught me to love you.

THE TOUCH

I like the way Jamaica makes me feel
when she touches my skin, it feels intemats like
fi mi man's fingurs as him peel ripe fruit,
yuh no de sort that drips
when you handle dem!

A JAMAICAN'S REFERENCE TO TOURISM

Dem try fi teif di land,
dem a try fi barb wire di sea, di air.

Red lobster besets our coast line
all red with the heat. Fat from
plenty.
Don't they know our water
is more than salt?
The sun more than shine,
more than holiday boasting.
This land holds the secrets of our ancestors.
De sort of secrets dat meek yuh proud,
like your Sunday clothes.

Red lobsters make such demands,
with tongues from Alabama, New York and Washington
while we, who have had to serve to survive,
still ask politely?

"Can I gets yuh a drink, sir?"

I, standing and waiting,
Lobster shows no recognition of my presence.
Turns on a smile, beams like
the conquistadors discovering a land not lost.
The ones who held Bible and gun in hand.
Looking me up and down only to say,

"When I'm in deep conversation, gyal,
don't disturb."

'Fucking Bastard, Pussy Clart,'
Screams in my head.
I hold out his glass of lime juice,

"Sir, I will take note of your request
on my next approach."

Full hip, bottom rolling, I turn and walk away.
Remembering the school fees due Monday, the rent too,
and a bill from h'every odda backside
 who wants a piece of my soul.

Lobster reached out for the glass of liquid; cold, cool, refreshing.
Taking a sip of his lime juice,
a strange, cloudy, yellowy green today.
She who had served the lobster all week,
smiled to herself and took her leave.

A MAD YOU WANT TO MAD ME

Remember, it's not madness if you see mi laugh,
it's just mi need fi sort out my own walk,
find mi way fi survive this journey and tek more tea breaks.

WAY OF THE OLD AFRICAN

To my oldest sister, Georgina, who is the truest
purest meaning of grace.

I have been a Jamaican all my life.
On the night I was first conceived.
From the minute she pushed me out.
Her warm melodious voice hummed
with sugary memories of homeland tone.

I'm not English, well not until the warm
air licked my skin, heat wrapped around me,
I am in its cocoon.
I feel the oils of this place
raise to my surface,
the balm of welcoming.

The first beads of sweaty salty droplets
from my forehead, run to thick brown lips,
I am tasting myself.
I call to him that is in my roots.
And to she who held my seed in her womb.
I call to Arabella. I sing a praise song to her,
for the ground she tended, *dirt de tough.*
She existed as mother, grandmother, great grandmother.

Her voice, our counselling, long after she dead.
I hear her voice through her daughter,
my mother, so I pass her wisdom to my daughter.
I hear her welcome me home.
I hear acknowledgement that I am part
of her and she of me.

Papa David, some called you Uncle D,
I call to you,
I call because I must,
I call for he was my wash water of love,
stern father, seeker of knowledge,
not afraid to correct, holds no fool's corner.
His name father, grandfather and great grandfather.

I hold the picture of you, aged 29, in my heart.
So I teach my son of your insight,
taught by your daughter to me.
I pour the water to the ground and call
on those who seeded me a century ago,
I call on them to protect me.

I must do this libation,
I must call on those who have known me
in the pre-existence of one continued consciousness,
on all of those who have gone on.

I am whole, I am home.
I will seek you on the hillside
in the light of a new Jamaican dawn
and take my rest.

MY MAMA'S SUITCASE

In her suitcase was the love she nurtured
for this place she called home.
Stories of duppy dawg[4] who walked grandma
from Spanish Town to Bog Walk.
Warning her of a stranger man
on de same road home,
whilst telling us little children
how she wouldn't want to encounter a rolling calf.[5]

She told us how she loved eating papaya, star apples
and guinep. Having trupance,
to buy a bag of mint balls,
six large paradise plums.
Two of which should always be inna yuh mouth,
and how trupance bought coffee and bread
and tobacco for Papa as well.

She told us how she learnt the Charleston
and the black bottom, how hers
was one much sought after and loved.
Mama said that she loved herself,
cause grandmother told her to
and taught us to do the same.
She said there was no tree or twig in her face
and that she was Sista Beautiful
and so were we.

She told tales of shallow rivers to cross
on your way to school, stepping stones
in warm river water.

Carrying your only good pair of shoes
around your neck, tied by the laces.

She spoke of St. Mary where Papas people deh come from,
Obia men, women who practice science,
Anansi's cunning stories.

[4] 'duppy dawg' is a ghost dog

[5] A 'rolling calf' is the spirit of a dead butcher

HAVE A STRATEGY

A man fi know when it's time fe siddung an be quiet!
She said,
make your moves like you a play chess.
At all times, try fi have a strategy!
Sometime you fi count di cost before you mount your
jackass.
She said monkey do as monkey see!
She said,
liquor had a spirit at its heart,
it is where demons are lurking, an tun you fool!
In God there is no condemnation but Him said, sin no
more!
Grace is for those who are willing fi let de most high change
dem!
I ask are you willing?
I know I am, only sometimes though!

TEACH ME FATHER

This sphere that is our physical cosmos,
is surrounded by ether above the earth,
between earth and below.
That which is in the non-existent is him and I.
Somewhere in between is God.
Don't let intellect divorce God from you
under the guise that says He is indulgent,
temporal, provocative or brazen.
Know you are made from 13 elements,
all of which come from the dust,
whence you came and where you return.

PHILOSOPHER AND FATHER [6]

For my brothers and sisters: our Dad.

He spoke of sorrel wine and fish on a Friday,
of rice and peas, his mother's - our grandmother's -
sweet potato pudding, his knowledge of cricket
and Sir Garfield Sobers.

He spoke of dancing to John Holt on a Saturday night,
brandy shorts and Guinness, holding his woman right,
and how it reminded him of home: of jukeboxes, reggae
and mento music vibrating off roof tops,
the blessed assurances that came from the churches
on every street corner, and listening to Jim Reeves
on a Sunday.

There were times life and love treated him hard
in this cold place. He said try to be who you are,
be true to yourself - it's what was taught him,
it was his philosophy. Even if life punched ugly wounds.
So he cooked and he played and he danced
to his own rhythms.
In those movements his children were conceived.

[6] First published in *Sweet Tongues: Crocus Book of Food Poems*, Crocus Books

SHE WROTE HER OWN EULOGY

KEEPING YOUR OWN COUNSEL

Let no one person know everything about you.
Keep something back about yourself,
for barren times approacheth, without warning.
And that's when your own counsel is important.

MELTED GREY

Six stones or 84 lbs, if you're from the USA.
She is now a feather's weight.
Once she had been my
Mohammed Ali, my heavyweight champion.

A white pail stood in the corner of her room,
its lid on to conceal its golden contents.
I sometimes wondered had she peed
her entire body weight away.

The bottle of cus cus perfume was overpowering
like the paraffin lamps of old.
I don't know, what flowers it was made from
it was a sickly, syrupy smell filling her room.

One of her grandchildren had spilt it a while back,
it ominously lingered in the air,
mixed with the smell of her pee
and flatulence.
She once said, "Death has a smell you know."

My Grandmother's portrait pervaded the room,
like a warning of a beating yet to come.
There were no tunes playing
just me rattling on about some new group I was listening to,
"Sweet Honey in the Rock" or was it "Boy George"?

She was not listening and didn't much care anymore
about anything,
other than the constant reminder that she was tired.

Yet she was in bed.
I didn't get that she was tired.
Tired from what?

The youngest child, always in full flow,
She said, "For GOD'S SAKE shut up pickney."
I laughed, how quick her mouth could be.
Her temper was Scotch Bonnet,
frustration lacing the air.

She shouted and cussed all of us
on whatever day you happened to be there.
I struggled to make her laugh
and caught my reflection in her mirror,
opening the pill box.
In that instant I saw the truth
that I could end her tired,
I pondered on the cocktail of medicine.
Then I didn't,
because my grandmother was looking on from her
position on the wall,
looking into my soul.

JUNIPER AND TEARS

I walk on pathways of juniper
and my mother's tears.

In my delusion,
I thought your arms were safety.
Believing you would look after her
like the jewel she was;
You buried my laughter and smiles;
she bruised, easily.
But she was your minimum wage.
You had more clients than
your eight-hour day.

Mama said, "How can you see
and not sympathise? You too will grow old."

Now I walk alone, retracing my steps.
Remembering stolen words, the fluttering of her fingers.

WHEN MAMA SPOKE OF HER PAINS

I called at Mama's last night, to put my mind to rest
before I went home to sleep.
She was awake, restless, as I washed her face with
a warm flannel. she said:

Mi nearly dead last night
don't you care
mi nearly dead last night you were not there
the grim reaper came
mi hav fi run him out of town.
Mi? Mi not ready fi going down.
I nearly dead last night
but had to stick around
mi no ready
fi wear no deadman crown
no deadman crown, no deadman crown.
Oh glory come, but not now
mi nearly dead last night
and you never asked how or why
you come a mi house
just a siddung
a cry,
you like fi tell me fi you troubles and trials
but when mi tell fi mine
you always have no time
you never came to stay
is what you always say.
Pickney stop hold mi hand
listen and hear
just let mi share

that life no sweet now
mi feels mi heart string a go bruk
and mi belly it always a jump up
mi in a pain and last night in dis ya bed -
the sweat poured down from mi head.
I nearly called to the Lord
tek mi now.
Mi nearly dead last night
but suddenly it came to mi
I no ready, you can't have mi
I'm not for no heavenly blues
or angelic wings chorus to sing.
If truth be known I have people to see
from May Pen to Spanish Town
(keep holding my hand)
I got six pickney fi order round
Caribbean meals on wheels fe cuss
but not Miss Thomas, she always look bout mi
no heavenly bound bus, no pearly gates to see.
I want to stay a little longer just pain free, no rain ago suss on mi
(keep holding my hand)
so death see mi here
you just can't have mi
so death se mi here
you just can't have...

I placed her in bed and drove home with the wipers on.
When I got out of the car I realised it wasn't raining, the water
was in my eye.

STRICT INSTRUCTIONS - JOURNAL

I held her aqua silk bound book in my hand,
the scent of my mother's Charlie perfume on its cover.
The date of all our birthdays,
all ten of us, our birth signs,
as if to remind her of our characteristics.
Doodles and sketches of places I'd never seen,
a love heart and a pressed buttercup
were amongst her private thoughts.
Its pages are where we might know her now.

My Mother's journal left us strict instructions:
On my death, try fe make mi look good,
the cream suit should be the one you put me in—
I like the length of the skirt. Put on mi good shoes,
I don't want fe meet mi maker wid mi naked bare foot dem.

Choose the songs for the church wisely,
I like Psalms 23 and I did like Rod Stewart's
"Don't you think I'm sexy". That will shock a few.
There will be those who mourn loudly
but didn't love me. That's okay, it's dem conscience.

Cry if you must, but know it was my end.
Smile if you can, cause I did love
each and every one a you de same.
Remember me, my voice,
it's my mother's and her mother's and is yours now,
it's how I bear losing my own mother in 1962.
I made mistakes, it's the way of this life and it's alright,
remember I grow you with faith.

It will become important at the hours of my passing.

Love one another—
Be mindful of each other, for there are those
who will try fe set you against each other.
Don't fight fe money,
I set aside a little something fe all of unu.

All that I am you are,
you are the voice of my mother,
the knowing of my father,
all the sistas and brothers of your lineage
from David to Arabella and those that withstood the storms.

P.S. buy me a good headstone - one befitting of your mother.

GATHER UNTO ME I SAY

This poem is dedicated to my daughter, Nicole, who
asked me a question at a Nine Night.

Gather unto me I say,
those of you who wear the black cloth perpetual.
Midweek and always on Friday.
You became a partaker of the ritual
when you became fettered to the nine nights,
and a frequent visitor to the house of the dead.

Gather unto me all
who have embraced the idea of the gathering,
for it gains momentum, when the first call goes out,
to Aunty church woman and brother man shubeens,
she brings the brethren, unto herself at first.
She comes with Bible.
They hold the rod of correction
in love. In the hope to save one soul.

He comes with the fire of Wray and Nephew,
Cain White, it burns the back of your throat, a different hot.
His tongue is laced with bumboclaat, rassclaat redemption.
He too makes the call.
They come with ivory domino and embers of fire.
Like soothsayers and mystics, they come
with the knowledge to read the cards in your hand.
They are the men, the women
who can find the 6 6 6 you hold.
He comes with the herb of Solomon,
Rizla, matches, and no regrets.

The two come together, sinner and saint,
they eye each other suspiciously,
there they tell stories and reminisce of good days and bad.
Of church outings and blues parties, of summers and winters.
They be laughing about the coach trips to Skegness,
with rice and peas and curry goat in the dinner flasks.

Someone raises the song,
"We shall gather by the river."
While someone shouts, "6."
As the domino crashes on Mama's best dining table,
this is the only time
she does not have the screw face of resistance.
We take more moments to drink and to groan,
to mourn, to cry.
We pour over old photographs laughing
at the clothes we wouldn't wear today.
We see images, of images, our dead, our living together,
reminding us how the time we have together,
is short, is short, is short.

Mama said live, love and do
but don't stray far from the old ways of we people—
for it is important to gather unto yourselves.

DE WHOOP AND HATE

Blood, blues, bleeding, into bold women.
speaking and singing songs of de-whoop
breathing metallic mustard gas, burning you inside,
only seeing on the outside a dead smile.
Wild, reckless dancing, to music
appropriated from ancestral rites,
they are the ones who refused to lay still like the dead.

They were airborne yet wingless.
They danced until feet were blooded blues,
bending but never buckling, under rash, berating, brutes.
They wielded cutlasses rusted over time,
lay still like sentries with locked gates,
moving in the realms of angels and demons.

They were preachers singing prophetically
with their children strapped to their backs.
Surviving winters harsh, springs wet and insipid.
Stinking summers of more lost blood and the falling
monotony of an autumn life,
that was never theirs to possess.

The prophetess waxed lyrical with songs of mend your ways
and find forgiveness within, as though throats were not
raw from crying out for deliverance.
Songs that would become folklore,
changed over time to suit another agenda
as archaeologists would find bones and fill in sentences
with their own truths.
So in time, even this story, would have a new interpretation.

They dream for their children, big not small
they saved for their children's futures
from the little they did not own.
They moved the mountains and stood deep in shit
while telling their children better times
were around the corner.

ALL ABOUT POWER

Village compounds
dogs barking
babies crying
my grandmother's hand
guiding me. Which one
of my grandmothers
came to me and held me
I will never know,
both had passed long
before my birth.

She was in yesterday's
dreams. Guiding me back
from a precipice
with strong words in my ear.
Her arms my DNA.
I was raised with her love
and the memory of her. Of them.
Unlike the forest and flora of Senegal and Cameroon
ripped from my throat, no longer home.

I have a knowledge that cannot be ripped from me
that place on the hill with head tied women
girding up their waists in red silk and white cotton
dancing a free dance of the Southern Bantu forest and
mountain people.
Their songs, their earth are a part of me
a forced seasoning couldn't change this!

AS WATER SWIRLS

I sing to you my words.
Hammering them, chanting them—
melodic tones of my philosophies.
My words wash like warm water on troubled times.
The sound of my voice is both ancient and new.
It echoes the cries of women sold into marriages
and the Sista that is circumcised for sexual pleasure,
my words surge round dungeons dug deep underground
for daughters, by fathers: I will rage, shout for our freedoms.
My word is bound to the earth.
It is love, it is *Dunamis* power this voice of mine.
I will fight, we will together overcome devastation.
The words live in me, it calls to the deep.
Hear my words, cradle them, keep them close.
My word must call you from apathy to militancy,
from complacency to revolution. They must
cause your soul to search like the prophets searched for God.

My words float on waterfalls,
With an elegance,
soft and reminiscing,
Within the words lies the healing balm
of my mother's voice, and her mother's voice, and her
mother's voice...

MY GRANDMOTHER'S STORY

TOMORROW[7]

We stand in all our yesterdays,
where the valiant had once stood.
Where heroes now stand,
we will not flinch nor fall.
For we have come too far.
So we battle like
Queens should.
Mothers called to combat
like the battalions of our families,
all those who did not lie down
whilst others took possession
of our rise and fall.
Spirited like our mother's mother
and our mothers before.
We did not yield ground,
but braced ourselves for the journey
in hulls of tall ships to distant shores.
Bejewelled cargo of victors and brave women.
We are the jet black fabulous jazz of isosceles,
we stand in all our yesterdays.

Where the valiant had once stood
where heroes now stand,
you set a path for us to ascend
to find the very best in us,
as we enter the city gates,
we are people that have battled,
against those who, would try to defeat us.

[7] First published in Catching Hell and Doing Well, UCL IOE Press / Trentham Books

You made us strong , you gave us your voice
you left us with your songs, told us to rise,
on the dawn, and to overstand the storms,
you made us spirited,
we are Kenya, Egypt,
Senegal, Rwanda,
Mali, Libya,
Madagaskar, Nigeria,
Jamaica, Barbados, we are Trinidad
we people called to arms, a people
not afraid.
So we stand in our yesterdays,
where the valiant had once stood
and we claim all our tomorrows
in this our victory.

CLOSE TO THE PIT

Dark and light.
These are the elements of my life.
For a time I stood close
to the edge.
Then I realised,
that I was worth more than the broad mile
where neon lights
artificial in their glow
would pull you to their thrones.
It shines unnatural light
had no shadow no conscience
no afterglow.
Hell lurks there just waiting silently.
I heard the screams!
The cries that no human was supposed to hear.
My spirit heard them though,
still like the fool forward I go.
Recognising. Hearing it!
I would have heard no warning voice
for you first need to be silent...
And listen to that inner spirit, your ancestors.
Nevertheless, laced with wine and a spirit of a different kind
onwards I went.
So potent was its draining power
the broad mile with neon light glow.
I chose not to recognise its sting
deadly like the poisonous toxins.
We now breathe in but call air,
looking for what does not want to found.
Seeking in others what is, lacking in yourself.

Then blaming your own destruction
on not knowing
when all time that voice inside scream "No."
For a time I stood close to the edge.
For a time I stood close.

GRANDMOTHER KNEW HOW TO LOVE - PART 1

For Naomi Clarke and all of the Clarkes.

David, my browning, I took much from you, di man
who give me twelve children, one dead lef' eleven
and I did bawl fe de loss of that one.
I raise all of your sons and nurtured your daughters.

Kept sacred secrets, just in case they encountered
hard hearts, who couldn't understand. To dis love,
I did yield and it was more than thirteen times.

Each child I named, each a line furrowed deep
in my brow. Each one of you reminds me
of my belly pain, twelve children, one dead, lef' eleven.

To my first, the twins Alice and Gladys,
I surrendered to the pure love of your tiny hands and feet.
The explosion you caused in my heart.

You girls made me want Bertram and Mordecai,
my first sons. Men of stature is my hope for them.
Born in the likeness of their father, they will be.

Then came Naomi and Edith, you two will be more than me—
I will teach you both the art that is home,
where love will pour from you.
You are devoted daughters and Sistas—
and will become devoted mothers.

Oscar, my boy, sweet, thoughtful, good man.
Jehovah will be your shield, your portion

and by His name your neighbour will know Him.

Arnold, a man of few words, you are kindness and foresight.
You, a carpenter, born on Christmas Day, my Merry man!
A loyal father, home maker—unlike many a man.

Gladstone my boy, Papason, ya mother dead,
so I mind you and love you like you were my own belly pain.
You will be wisdom, you will hear the Most High call you prophet.

When my last two were born, Ella and Victor,
I never knew I would have any love left,
for this life was not easy.
You both overwhelm my heart, so I promise love will follow you,
not rain. Test this love—
it will grow in you like morning dew fresh every day.

Each one of you is mine and David's,
I surrendered these calloused hands
to the raising of you, our children.
You were made from alabaster, mahogany, and the love
that that engulfs a mother's heart.

So I dreamed big for our children, my children.
I hold life in dis yah water jar, pray that the rain don't come
and pray the rain don't come and pray the rain don't come.

GRANDMOTHER KNEW HOW TO LOVE - PART 2

It wasn't dat mi did want to leave, to go—
it was just dat mi couldn't take any more.
It was not Kingston, where my love was,
it was right there in Harker's Hall, St Catherine.
It was right there, in we bed, where
familiar hands knew my breast, my belly.
I knew of the place in the small of your back
that made you still at my touch.

My hands, my mouth traced the steel muscles of your thighs,
where I had tasted the salt on your skin.
I had feasted on your tongue of rum and strong herbs.
I knew every inch of you and you of me—
yet still, I was not enough. I gave myself to you,
before we were obligated by rings and the preacher
and our families.
I was yours beneath a July Meridian skies,
bound by the labour of our hands,
we worked the field together
laugh and turn fool fi each other.
I, the fleshy pulp of sweet guinep
guava to your ravenous thirst,
only you wanted to mad me, turn mi fool
with this love ting, mek mi bawl.

It seems you prefer June plum, green and acidic on your tongue
you try fi turn my countenance from joy to
a sour face black woman.
You, who give me twelve children, one dead lef' eleven,
I raise all of your sons and nurtured your daughters.

Kept sacred secrets, just in case they encountered
hard hearts, who couldn't understand. To dis love,
I did yield and it was more than thirteen times.

Mi modda always did worn mi, fe staywa
from certain Stary-eyed bwoy for dem change, just like green
lizard in high grass.
You who is made from alabaster, mahogany, and bakra blood
and his last name.
I, Arabella, hold life in this water jar,
hoping dat de rain don't come,
but de bad bitch came, just as I did.
Give you three more children
to add to our twelve
and I could not hate them
and I refused to hate her
and you had made *me* yours and you had made *her* yours
until I found my senses in the naming of my children.
So I left you for Kingston, and my children
and your children.

I will keep a little oil in my kerosene lamp for me
so I can see straight, fi brighten my way to glory,
I will not be filled with hate because of you.

PROMISE OF WISDOM BORN FROM FOLLY

He had not wanted to fall in love
for this would show his vulnerability,
the lack of his iron control.
For he sat at the feet of the master
who informed him that his discipline
was never to fall.
So, when she breezed in like minted water
crisp, sharp, new.
Hibiscus for her perfume,
lips fat with the promise of death and light
from their loving.
All he did was remember the master's word,
this left him destined to have no captive heart—
although passionate lover he could be.
His mind needs its own solitude,
he took what was on offer.
held no fast,
she on the other hand would not at first be put off,
from the length he went to keep her
on the outside of his inner being.
She came with her own game plan
no longer wearing hibiscus perfume
to lure him in,
she wore the fragrance of her sex,
and still he did not succumb,
never answered her calls,
never eats at her table,
bought no presents,
never revealed his involvement
with her to others.

As she is wisdom and folly her playground,
she learnt not to sell herself short
recaptured her own heat
and now stands.

Where there is no fuel a fire goes out.[8]

[8] *Proverbs 26:20*

WITH ME

For Winston and Alex: two men alike in more ways than one.

Alone, not lonely,
he whispered words.
Not enough
the obstacle-himself,
kneeling bowed in prayer,
his defence's down
he roared inside.
Yet he kneeled, motionless,
except for the single tear running down.

Sharing nothing, not even his whispered words.
Just him, the Alpha and Omega bound
together in prayer.
Alone yet not on his own, his defences down
he roared inside
his whispered words, whispered words.

YOU MUST BECOME A CARTOGRAPHER

For Alexander and Nicole May.

The sun has gone down for the night,
there is a yellow haze riding the sky,
the day is slowly slipping into a warm grey,
dark indigo blue the melody of this Friday,
the TV invasion switched off.

The sound the clock makes could be thunder right now,
it weighs heavy on this silence I yield to.
It reminds me that no one can guarantee you a life without
firework
and rollercoaster trials.
So take some time to order some things.
I say to my son and daughter—buy yourselves a compass
and a notebook and make your own map.

If it was not for the oldest grandchild, Jemmett, and his wife, Mavis Clarke, and their retelling of our story, it would be lost in this new world. "Without the knowledge of our past, how do we shape our future?"

This is an African-Jamaican story.

THE END